BY BARBARA DE ANGELIS, Ph.D.

Books

ARE YOU THE ONE FOR ME?
ASK BARBARA: The 100 Most Asked Questions About Love,
Sex, and Relationships
*CONFIDENCE: Finding It and Living It
HOW TO MAKE LOVE ALL THE TIME
*INSPIRATIONS ABOUT LOVE
*101 WAYS TO TRANSFORM YOUR LOVE LIFE (flip book)
REAL MOMENTS
REAL MOMENTS FOR LOVERS
THE REAL RULES: How to Find the Right Man for the Real You
SECRETS ABOUT MEN EVERY WOMAN SHOULD KNOW

Audiocassettes

* FINDING LOVE
* CONFIDENCE: Finding It and Living It
* MAKING RELATIONSHIPS WORK
* MAKING LOVE WORK
PASSION

(All of the above are available at your local bookstore.
Items marked with an asterisk may also be ordered
by calling Hay House at 800-654-5126.)

❧   ❧   ❧

Please visit the Hay House Website at: **www.hayhouse.com**

CONFIDENCE

CONFIDENCE

Finding It and Living It

Barbara De Angelis, Ph.D.

Hay House, Inc.
Carlsbad, CA

Copyright © 1995 by Barbara De Angelis

Published and distributed in the United States by:

Hay House, Inc., P.O. Box 5100, Carlsbad, CA 92018-5100
(800) 654-5126 • (800) 650-5115 (fax)

Edited by: Jill Kramer
Designed by: Christy Salinas

The author of this book does not dispense medical advice or prescribe the use of any technique as a form of treatment for physical or medical problems without the advice of a physician, either directly or indirectly. The intent of the author is only to offer infor-mation of a general nature to help you in your quest for emotional well-being and good health. In the event you use any of the information in this book for yourself, which is your constitutional right, the author and the publisher assume no responsibility for your actions.

Library of Congress Cataloging-in-Publication Data

De Angelis, Barbara.
     Confidence : finding it and living it / Barbara De Angelis.
       p. cm.
     ISBN 1-56170-528-4
     1. Self-confidence. 2. Trust (Psychology) I. Title.
BF575.S39D43   1995
152.4--dc20

                           95-11222
                           CIP

ISBN 1-56170-528-4

01 00 99 98   7 6 5 4
First Printing, October 1995
Fourth Printing, October 1998

Printed in the United States of America

CONTENTS

❧ PREFACE ❧

You would never guess by looking at my life now, with all of its successes and notoriety, that I used to have absolutely no confidence in myself. The truth is: I entered adulthood as a frightened, insecure young woman who was afraid to discover my own dreams, let alone attempt to make them come true. That's why I did not even begin my present career until after I turned 30. It took me that long to find my own source of power and confidence within.

As a teacher and a pathfinder, I am constantly asked questions such as:

"How did you get to be so confident?"

"Can you give me suggestions for developing my own self-confidence?"

"What has contributed the most to your feelings of confidence and self-worth?"

The answers to these questions lie within the pages of this small but powerful book. Like all truths, the truth about living with confidence is very simple, and yet very profound. Once you understand the true nature of confidence, you will be able to tap into your own source of infinite personal power that will fill you with more purpose and peace than you could ever have imagined possible.

I hope that what I've written will help you find your way back to the person you are meant to be.

— Barbara De Angelis
Los Angeles, California

THE SEARCH FOR TRUE CONFIDENCE

Do you ever find yourself thinking, *I would like to be more confident?*

Are you waiting to do certain things in your life *until* you feel more confident about yourself?

Are you postponing writing that book, or painting that picture, or starting a new career, or asking that desirable person out on a date until you feel better about yourself?

Are you sitting around doing nothing, or not doing as much as you'd like to, hoping that one day, the confidence you've been seeking will magically appear?

Do you ever suspect that, although you may have achieved a certain level of success and accomplishment in your life, underneath you still don't feel as confident and strong as you think you should?

This book is about confidence. The ideas about confidence I am going to share with you will probably be very different from those you've ever heard before. Most people don't understand the true meaning of the word *confidence,* and so they don't experience the kind of confidence that they really need in their lives. I attribute all of my success to my confidence, but not the kind of confidence that you traditionally think about. In fact, it wasn't until I began practicing this new kind of confidence that I was able to make my dreams come true.

In this book, I am going to reveal how you can find a source of so much confidence inside yourself that you will be able to do the things you've always wanted to do, and be the things you've always wanted to be. In fact, the moment you start to look at confidence differently, your life will begin to change. You don't have to wait ten years or five years—it can happen tomorrow!

I hope this book will help you to:

- **Understand what confidence really is;**

- **Find out what gives you (not everybody—but YOU, in particular) confidence;**

- **Learn what you may be doing in your life, without realizing it, to sabotage your confidence, and find out how to break those unhealthy habits; and**

- **Discover the keys to creating more confidence in your life.**

What Do You Think Confidence Really Is?

Most of us think that having confidence means believing in our ability to do certain things well. In other words, someone might say, "I'm an artist, and I have confidence in my ability to paint certain brush strokes, to be able to visualize objects and reproduce them on the canvas, to be able to get the colors right," and so on. Or, "I'm a salesperson, and I have confidence in my ability to know how to talk to people on the phone, to be able to close the deal, to influence others to buy my product." Or, "I'm a man, and I have confidence in my ability to get women to like me, and that means that I have confidence that I know how to impress someone on the first date, that I know how to make women happy, that I am a wonderful lover."

But there is a problem with believing that in order to be a confident person, you have to do something well, whether it's painting, selling, loving, cooking, or whatever. That problem is that:

There are only so many skills you can learn to master in life, only a limited number of abilities you can acquire. So, if your confidence in yourself is based on what you can do well, you will only feel confident part of the time, when you are doing that particular activity.

That means that if you're selling real estate, and you do it well, you will feel confident during the actual moment you sell a property, but the rest of the time, you won't. If you're skilled at helping others, whether as a friend or professional, you'll feel good about yourself in those moments when you're giving advice, or offering comfort, but the rest of the time, you won't. If you're a writer, you'll feel confident in those moments when you finish an article or book, and the rest of the time, you won't.

You can see that unless you spend ALL of your time doing the thing you are good at, and doing it in a way that satisfies you, you will limit the amount of time you can feel confident. This explains why so many people become *work*aholics, or *rescue*holics or become similarly obsessed with an activity that eats up too much of their time and creates imbalance in their lives—they only feel good about themselves when they're actively performing that job, task, or using that ability.

Confidence is something that ought to transcend what we know and what we do.

There are only so many things in life that you can do, and so many abilities that you can master. If you base your confidence on those things, you will never be a truly self-confident person. You'll only feel confident about those particular talents: "I feel confident that I'm a good computer programmer, and a good tennis player, and a good father to my kids...but I don't feel an all-pervading sense of confidence about myself."

Think about it: Have you ever achieved something wonderful, something you worked hard for, and *although you felt good about your **accomplishment**, you still didn't feel good about **yourself?***

Maybe you'd been going to college for four years wondering, Am I going to pass, am I going to be able to write these papers? Am I going do what it takes to graduate? And you worked and you worked, and finally, you stood there on graduation day, and strangely enough, you didn't feel satisfied. Perhaps you thought, Big deal, so now I have this piece of paper. I still don't feel really good about myself and confident that my future will turn out the way I want it to.

You see, if confidence just came from being a good student, writing those papers, getting the grades, you would have felt like a million dollars.

Here's another example: Imagine there was a job that you *really, really* wanted. You'd been working at all these other awful jobs, and finally, you get that position you've been dreaming of. Now you have your dream job, and you become successful in other people's eyes—and yet, you still don't feel really good about yourself? And you may say to yourself, "What's going on? I spent all this time and hard work getting here, and now that I'm here, I don't feel the way I think I should. I always believed that if I had this job, I'd feel so powerful inside, but I still feel the same as I did before."

If confidence came from your ability to acquire a certain position or to make a certain amount of money, that job or that raise would give you tremendous, permanent confidence. But confidence *isn't* that; many of us finally get the job that we yearn for, or make the money we want. We create the relationship we've always dreamed of. We buy the house we thought we never could, and we discover that we still don't feel confident.

Do You Ever Feel Like an Impostor?

There is a term in psychology that describes this experience of achieving success on the outside that we don't feel we deserve on the inside—it's called the *Impostor Phenomenon.* The Impostor Phenomenon means that no matter what we do, we feel like we've perpetrated a fraud. We say, "Oh, it was a fluke that I got this job. I have this job now, but if I had to start all over again, I couldn't do it. Somehow, it just happened." Or, "I don't know how I actually closed that big deal, but I can't imagine it could happen again. It was just a fluke." Or, "If people knew how incompetent I was, they wouldn't want me around. If my boss really knew what kind of job I was doing, she wouldn't respect me. If people really knew how I felt about myself inside, they wouldn't look up to me."

Sometimes we feel like impostors when, on the outside, we've achieved things that we feel should give us confidence, but on the inside, we don't feel confident at all.

No matter how much you achieve or acquire in life, if you don't have true confidence on the inside, then those external possessions or successes simply don't matter.

Now, perhaps you're not yet at a place in your life where you believe that what I'm saying could possibly be true. You may still be striving to achieve wealth and success; you may still be climbing up the mountain. And you may say to yourself, "If *I* had all the things I want, *I* would certainly be confident." Well, don't bet on it. I meet and work with people all the time who have more money than they could ever spend; they have achieved all the things that you would think would make them feel confident and happy with themselves. They are famous, respected, sometimes even worshiped, but they still don't feel confident. What do they need? What's the missing link?

The Nature of True Confidence

True confidence has nothing to do with what is happening in your outer life. True confidence isn't created because of *what* you do, but because of your belief in the ability *you have within* to do anything you want to.

True confidence is always generated from within, not without. *It comes from a commitment you make to yourself, a commitment that you will do whatever it is that you want and need to do in life.* **It is founded on a trust in you, not a trust in the outcomes you may or may not achieve.**

Confidence is a belief in your spirit as a person—that no matter what you are faced with in life, you will deal with it, and do what you need to do. It is not that you will *do* a certain thing; *it is your willingness to act.* If you believe in yourself as a person, then no matter what you are faced with, you will act and accomplish what you want. *So, it is not confi-*

dence in a particular ability you have, such as confidence in your being a good attorney, or being a good musician; it is confidence in your ability to take action in your life. Do you see the difference?

Like many people, I used to base my sense of confidence on what I did. If I achieved good results, I felt temporarily confident, but it only lasted until my next, not-so-good result, and then just as quickly as it came, that feeling of confidence would vanish. So if I gave a seminar and 500 people showed up, I would feel confident for the moment. But if only 70 people showed up, I'd feel deflated, and full of self-doubt. This same pattern would occur in all areas of my life—if one of my books sold a lot one week, I'd feel wonderful. If the next week, however, it dropped off of a bestseller list, my confidence would drop, too. What an emotional roller coaster! And yet this is the way so many of us live.

Here's the irony: *By basing my confidence on the response I got from the Universe to my goals and dreams, I was setting myself up to inevitably feel a lack of confidence!* After all, I can't control the way the Universe responds to me. I can't even logically believe that I will always get just the result I want in life—that's not the way the world works. And so I certainly cannot count on always receiving a positive response to my efforts.

But there is one thing I can count on: I can count on my own commitment to *myself*—to be true to my desires and take the action necessary to help manifest those desires. I can count on my own determination to know what I need to do and do it. And that's what I can have confidence in. **I have confidence in my ability to do whatever it takes.**

Will what I do always work out in my favor? Of course not. Will I achieve everything I set out to do? The answer is no. But that's all right, because I won't be basing my confidence on the outcome I receive. My confidence will have its genesis in the fact that I did what I did, just as I said I would.

When you base your confidence on who you are, instead of what you accomplish, you have created something that no one or no circumstance can ever take away from you.

Here's another reason that true confidence cannot grow out of what you accomplish. No matter how good you get at doing something, you will only gain confidence about your ability to do that particular thing. So when you attempt to do something new, something you aren't skilled at, your old confidence will be useless, since you won't have any confidence about your ability to do that new thing well.

I remember going through this years ago when I decided to write my first book, *How to Make Love All the Time*. I was a very successful seminar leader, and I felt what I thought was confidence about my ability to attract people to a seminar and take them through a powerful weekend. But I had never written a book before, and I was scared to death! I remember thinking, Sure, I know how to put on a powerful seminar, but I have absolutely no idea how to write a good book. Where do I begin? What if I can't finish it? What if people think it's stupid?

All of my confidence about being a successful seminar leader couldn't make a dent in my fear about becoming a writer—*the confidence didn't translate from one activity to another.*

Why was I so scared? It wasn't because I hadn't written a book before. I was scared because at the time, I was not operating from a place of true confidence in myself. I still believed that I couldn't develop confidence about doing a particular task— in this case, writing a book—until I had become competent at that task. It actually took writing that first book (which has become a national bestseller), for me to realize that I didn't know what true confidence was, because when it came time to write the second book, I thought, Surely now that my first book was a success, I won't be scared writing the next one. Well, guess what? I *was* scared. My mind was full of thoughts like, *So what if the first book was successful. This book is about a different topic. Maybe you won't be able to write about this topic as well as you wrote about the first. What if people don't like this topic as much.* And on and on.

It's taken me a long time and a lot of work on myself to find and stay connected with my true source of confidence. My confidence doesn't come from believing that I am a good writer who can make the bestseller list, or a successful seminar leader who can attract thousands of people to my lectures, or an infomercial star who can win awards. These achievements fill me with satisfaction and pride in my work, but they don't give me confidence. My confidence comes from knowing that if I decide to do something, I will do it.

I don't feel confident because I am smart. I feel confident because I know I will study and learn all I have to in order to get the job done. I don't feel confident because I know I can write a great book about anything. I feel confident because I believe in my commitment to sit down at the computer, and write, and tear up what I wrote, and write some more, and show what I wrote to people, and cry when they say it's not good enough, and write some more, until I finally get it right.

My real confidence is born of my will and my determination. I have confidence in my will as a person, that if I want to do something, I will learn about it. I will try over and over again, making mistakes and learning from them until I feel good about how I'm performing my new task. And even if what I do turns out wonderfully, it won't be the source of my true confidence. My confidence will come from knowing I had the determination to do whatever it took to get me where I wanted to go.

✂　　✂　　✂　　✂

CHAPTER TWO

HOW TO STOP SABOTAGING YOURSELF AND START TRUSTING YOUR DREAMS

Think about this question for a minute: If I gave you a job to do right now, no matter what it entailed, would your first reaction be, "Oh, I don't know if I can do that; I don't trust myself"? What if the job or assignment included activities you'd never done before? Would you feel excited about undertaking the challenge, or would you feel fear? Would you trust yourself to do whatever it took to learn the skills you needed to get the job done?

Is there a dream that you have right now, something important that you would like to do, but you don't totally trust that if you started working towards it, you would go the whole 100 yards? Are you afraid that you might get sidetracked, or procrastinate, and simply stop? Are there ventures (and adventures) in your life that you've begun, yet failed to complete?

The point at which you stop going forward with a dream is the point at which you have a break in confidence. It's the place where you don't trust yourself.

When your mind says, "I don't think I can do that," what you are really saying is: *"I don't trust myself* to learn, to study, to do what it takes to make my dream come true." The more you trust in your determination and commitment to do what it takes, the more confidence you will experience. **And having confidence means trusting yourself to push past those points of fear, and not giving in.**

I'm sure you've read stories about a person who started a company from nothing and became incredibly successful. Maybe a man developed a fried chicken business in some small town, eventually franchised it, and made $20 billion. When you hear about this guy, you think, Boy, was he lucky! He was just at the right place at the right time! Well, what you don't hear is how many mistakes he made—how many times he made poor investments, how many times he had to start all over again, how many times he came up against a great obstacle and thought he would never make it past.

What did this billionaire have that most of us don't? **He trusted himself to keep going no matter what.** He wasn't always sure how he'd forge ahead, or if he was going about it the right way. But he knew one thing: he wasn't going to stop. He had confidence that he wouldn't stop—even when he made mistakes.

You Have to Look Bad
Before You Can Look Good

If you're the kind of person who doesn't like to look bad, you're going to have a difficult time creating true confidence. That's because confidence isn't built on the belief that you know you will always look good, and avoid mistakes, but rather, on your willingness to look bad and keep going forward anyway. I'm a perfect example of this same principle. Most people think I'm very successful. All they see are the goals I've achieved. But what you're not seeing are the hundreds and hundreds of mistakes I've made in my life. I'm not talking about small mistakes, either—I mean really big ones: terrible errors in hiring employees; poorly conceived business decisions; the wrong choices in intimate partners...the list goes on and on. Now that I'm at a very happy, successful place, it might appear that it's all been a wonderful ride, but nothing could be further from the truth.

When I share my life story with people, they usually respond by asking, "How did you manage to have *any* confidence when all of these terrible things happened to you? Where did you get the confidence to pursue your dreams?" The answer is that I didn't have confidence that I *knew* what I was doing; *I didn't have confidence that I knew the answers. But I did have confidence that if I kept trying, I would figure out what I was doing eventually. I trusted myself to keep going.*

So, if you're reading this book, and you realize you've been waiting to feel like an expert before you begin something, waiting for the confidence to unfold, I'm telling you right now: **DON'T WAIT ANYMORE!** The only way to become "it"—whatever "it" is—is to be foolish about it for a long time first. You'll no doubt make tons of mistakes, and if you do that long enough, believe me, you will get better. Some of us are waiting to waltz in and do it perfectly the first time, and until we can do that, we just don't do *anything*, and that is called *pride*—pride and ego. So we don't do things that we aren't good at, and we keep doing the same things that we are good at, even though it's boring and not very fulfilling after a while. Then we wonder why we're not getting anywhere!

To succeed, you have to do something and be very bad at it for a while. You have to look bad before you can look really good.

When I first began writing, I was awful. My first manuscript came back from the editor with red slash marks on every other word. It was embarrassing. I was humiliated. But that's how I learned. The next book had fewer marks, and now, my books are published with little or no editing. *I had to be a terrible writer before I could become a successful writer.*

The same is true of my television career. Whenever I'm approached by someone who asks me my secret for becoming so confident and effective on television—someone who is afraid that they can never achieve that same confidence—I tell them to find a copy of the first television show I ever appeared on. This tape is awful. I'm mumbling; my thoughts are jumping all over the place; I'm wearing the wrong colors, and I don't smile once! It's so painful, I can hardly watch it myself, but from time to time I do. Seeing where I started reaffirms my trust in myself, in my confidence that I can get to where I want to go if I'm just willing to look bad for a while.

Are You Sabotaging Yourself by Waiting to Act?

I know that you have some dreams in your life right now. Maybe you want to start your own business. Maybe you want to go back to school and change careers. Maybe you want to write a screenplay. You can feel the desire burning inside of you. But the truth is, you aren't doing much about it. Why is that? Your mind answers with excuses:

"Well, I'm not sure how to go about it."
"This isn't a good time."
  And, of course: "I don't feel confident
    enough yet."

Most people I know wait until they feel confident before starting a project or going after a dream, and by doing so, they make a crucial mistake.

If you wait until you feel confident to do something new or go after a dream, you'll wait forever.

How are you going to gain confidence writing if you won't even sit down at your computer or typewriter? How are you going to gain the confidence to run a business if you're spending all your time on the sofa watching TV? How are you going to gain the confidence to have a relationship if you're staying home by yourself every weekend and avoiding people? You won't!

So many of us are hoping that a magical transformation will suddenly occur that will give us the courage to go out and change our career, or change our relationship, or take a chance. We're waiting for this mysterious influence to remove our fear and inspire us to go forward. How long have you been waiting for something to happen that will give you the courage and confidence you need to take action? I can tell you, you've been waiting too long. And it's not suddenly going to happen when you reach a certain age, or when the planets align in a certain way. You won't just suddenly wake up one day with this incredible sense of confidence you've been waiting for. In fact, the opposite will happen:

The longer you wait to go after your dreams, the less confidence you will have, and the fear that you'll never get what you want will become more intense.

This is how you can sabotage yourself without realizing it. The more you procrastinate about doing things you really want to do, whether they are personal or professional, the more immobilized you will become. And the more immobilized you are, the more frozen with fear, the more your confidence will be destroyed.

Are You Loving Yourself Conditionally?

Another consequence of procrastination is that you end up postponing the feeling of confidence and well-being you've been looking for by telling yourself: *"I will only feel good about myself when_____."* You fill in the blank. And, of course, that "when____" is something that you hope will happen in the future, something that is not occurring in the present. Therefore, you can't feel confident and positive about yourself in the moment.

Here are some common examples:

I WILL ONLY FEEL GOOD ABOUT MYSELF...

when I start my own business.

when I lose 20 pounds.

when I find a girlfriend or boyfriend.

when I'm making $50,000 a year.

when I'm totally out of debt.

when I can stand up to my mother.

when my husband and I feel close again.

when I get a promotion.

In other words, I'll feel good about myself, I'll feel confident, I'll love myself, *when* these requirements are met, and *until then, I'm not going to feel good about myself.*

There is nothing wrong with achieving things that make you feel good. Self-esteem is a natural by-product of accomplishment. **However, if you postpone feeling good about yourself *until* you achieve certain things, you are doing yourself a great disservice.** This is called *conditional self-love:* "I'll really feel good about myself when I can fulfill certain requirements, but until that time, I'm going to kick myself in the butt over and over again."

🦋   🦋   🦋   🦋

Imagine you're working for someone who assures you that you will get a bonus when you accomplish certain tasks. He gives you a list, and you run around doing everything he asked you to do. Finally, you're done, and when you come back to your boss, he says, "Oh, by the way, I forgot to tell you that there's another list of things you need to accomplish before you get your bonus."

If someone treated you this way, you'd be furious, wouldn't you? And yet we play this same game with ourselves all the time. "I'll feel good about myself," you say, "when I get that diploma, or start my business, or have those kids." But once we accomplish the goal, and wait for that great feeling of self-acceptance and confidence, we hear our own voice say, "I know I said this task was what I needed to love you, but actually, there's something else I need you to accomplish before I can feel really good about you."

⚹   ⚹   ⚹   ⚹

Have you ever been in a relationship with someone who loved you very conditionally? This person gives you one hurdle after another that you need to jump in order to win his or her love and approval. "Well, I can't make a commitment to you until you lose some weight," this person insists. So you lose the weight, and instead of the fulfillment you've been waiting for, you get a comment such as, "It's great that you lost the weight, but I'm not sure that we have the same values about our health. I really need you to change your diet." And so you change your diet, and of course, the inevitable happens: "Well, I know I said we'd get married when you got your body together, but to be honest, I'm concerned that you haven't done enough work on yourself emotionally." This person is stringing you along, which means that you're stringing yourself along, too.

If a friend told you this story, you'd probably respond by saying, "Dump him (or her). He's a jerk. I wouldn't put up with that kind of treatment from someone. Don't you see, nothing you do will ever be enough?" *But the sad truth is, you treat yourself in this same unloving way every time you postpone feeling good about yourself until you accomplish certain things.*

I have a good friend who recently told me a story about her husband that illustrates just what we're talking about.

> Bob is an attorney who loves to run. He has a goal of running a four-minute mile, and he believes that when he achieves that goal, he'll feel

great about himself. But right now, Bob can't run a four-minute mile. He can only run a five-minute mile. So every morning, he wakes up, goes for a run, and when he looks at his stopwatch, he gets depressed. He feels like a failure. He doesn't even enjoy running, because he is so fixated on making that four-minute mile.

Bob's wife complained to me that his goal of running a four-minute mile was affecting their relationship.

"Bob feels like a failure all the time," she confessed. "Every time I tell him how tired I am of seeing him unhappy, he comes back at me with: 'If I can just run a four-minute mile, everything will be great again. I just need to do this for myself.' " What Bob doesn't see is that he is loving himself very conditionally. He's set his sights on a goal he may or may not achieve. And instead of feeling confident because he commits to running every day and stays in good shape, he beats himself up.

Bob is ripping himself and his wife off. He has every reason to feel good about himself—his problem is that he doesn't understand what true confidence is. He isn't aware that he doesn't have to wait until he achieves a particular goal to feel confident. He can feel it and enjoy it right now.

Discover how you're sabotaging your sense of confidence.

In what ways are you postponing feeling good about yourself right now? What set of invisible criteria do you need to meet in order to feel confident? Do you really believe that when you achieve that goal or perform that task, you will feel great about yourself, and that the feeling of self-love will last? Well, it won't, because as we've seen, you can't maintain a constant level of achievement every minute of every day. And as soon as you reach one goal, it won't be enough, and you'll look to the next goal.

Here's an exercise that will help you pinpoint some of the ways you may be sabotaging your sense of confidence, and postponing loving yourself. Fill in the blanks with the first answers that pop into your head, and be as honest as you can.

"I'll feel really good about myself when...

_____."

"I'll feel really good about myself when...

_____."

"I'll feel really good about myself when...

_____."

"I'll feel really good about myself when...

_____."

"I'll feel really good about myself when...

_____."

"I'll feel really good about myself when...

_____."

It's amazing to do this exercise and discover all of the ways you might be unconsciously limiting your happiness and your sense of self-worth. Aren't you tired of it? Isn't it time to stop postponing loving yourself? Well, you can start making the change today. You don't even have to wait until you finish this book. Here's what I suggest:

Replace the thought: "I'll feel really good about myself when..." with the thought: "Right now, I feel really good about myself because..."

You might make a list with items such as these:

RIGHT NOW, I FEEL REALLY GOOD ABOUT MYSELF...

because I'm being honest with myself.

because I took good care of my body today.

because I reached out and asked for help from a friend.

because I expressed my feelings to my husband this morning.

because I was really there for my daughter when she needed me.

because I have the courage to read this book and face all my issues.

because I'm learning to love myself in the moment, just the way I am.

Doesn't that feel better than when you postpone acknowledging yourself until some time in the distant future?! You deserve to feel good about yourself right now, and *each time you honor yourself for being just where you are, you'll empower yourself to take your next step of growth and achievement.*

❧   ❧   ❧   ❧

HOW TO START BUILDING YOUR CONFIDENCE RIGHT NOW

The first step you need to take in order to build your confidence is to *stop pretending you're more confident than you actually are.* What does that mean? It means that you have to be honest about the ways you avoid facing your insecurities and ignore your dreams. It's not hard to trick yourself into believing that you do have a lot of self-confidence. How might you be doing that?

By putting a limit on how big you dream.

By being dishonest with yourself about your true needs.

By only doing things that don't challenge you.

By avoiding people or situations that do challenge you.

By telling yourself: "I don't care."

Imagine that you have a whole bunch of dreams piled up in your mind, dreams of all the things you want to do and experience in life. Let's say that some of the dreams in the pile will require only a little bit of confidence to achieve, and some of the more outrageous dreams will require a lot of confidence. If you don't have a lot of confidence, you'll look at that pile of dreams and say to yourself, "You know, I don't really care that much about these big dreams. I mean, they're not that important to me. I really only care about the dreams in this little pile over here. And I know I can accomplish these."

So you set out to achieve your small goals from the small pile, and conclude: "I really am a confident person. I don't have a problem with my self-esteem." But you're fooling yourself.

When you only set out to do what you already know you can do, you never develop a true sense of confidence.

This is how many of us cover up our lack of belief in ourselves—we dream small. By not wanting anything, by not needing anything, by not hungering for anything, we never have to fail, and therefore, we never have to face how little we believe in ourselves. We stop looking beyond the next mountain, and instead, tell ourselves that we are happy and full of confidence.

The truth is, when we dream small, we are ripping ourselves off. When we decide that things that secretly frighten or challenge us are not important, whether they be goals or relationships, we are lying to ourselves. And the false sense of confidence we achieve by not facing our fears will disappear with the first challenge we experience.

When You Limit Your Dreams, You Limit Your Life

If you don't have a dream in your head right now that scares you, then you've probably stopped dreaming. A lot of people stop dreaming because they don't believe in their ability to make their dreams come true, which is very convenient because then you can't fail, can you? Being afraid to fail doesn't indicate that something is wrong with you; having a dream that is scary doesn't mean that something's wrong with you—it simply means that you're human. I call that "healthy fear." But when you have dreams and do nothing about them all your life, and you let the fear paralyze you, that's not healthy.

Whenever I give lectures or seminars, I include a lengthy question-and-answer period at the end. One of the most frequently asked questions I hear goes something like this:

"Barbara, you've accomplished so much in your life, and done so many things that I'd be scared to death to do. How did you gain so much self-confidence and get rid of your fears?"

I love to shock my audience by answering:

"What makes you think I'm any less scared to death than you are?"

Once their nervous laughter settles down, I explain that, in spite of what they may think, my life is full of fear. Every time I undertake a new project, or commit to a new dream, I'm scared—scared of failing, scared of not doing it right, scared that I may be making a mistake. *But the difference between me and most other people is that I don't misinterpret the fear as a sign that I should stop doing what I'm doing. I don't use the fear as an excuse to not go forward.* In fact, when I'm feeling nervous or frightened, it usually means that I'm really stretching myself out of my comfort zone and into new directions—in other words, it usually means that I'm doing great!

So my confidence doesn't come from not having any fear. It comes from trusting that **in spite of my fear, I am going to act**; I am going to take one step after another towards my goal.

**True confidence doesn't come
from your not having any fear. It
comes from trusting yourself to
act *in spite of* your fear.**

Perhaps you've been misinterpreting your fear
as a sign of weakness, or as a lack of readiness.
When you make that mistake, you'll stay stuck
where you are in life, and will probably never find
true fulfillment.

If I waited until my fear disappeared before I
could go ahead and pursue my dreams, I'd still be
waiting. If I waited until my fear vanished before I
could go ahead and write a book, you wouldn't be
reading these words. If I waited until I conquered
my fear of getting hurt in a relationship before I
could go ahead and love again, I wouldn't be happily married today.

Don't let your fear of failure limit how you live.
**The presence of fear just means that you have big
dreams, and the bigger the dreams, the bigger
the fear.** Acknowledge your fear, and then act in
spite of it. The confidence you experience will come
from knowing you made your vision bigger than the
fear that accompanied it.

The Difference Between Confidence and Ego

Before we go on, let's address a concern you may have about becoming a really confident person. Some people, when they hear the word *confidence,* think of another word that tends to have a negative connotation, and that word is...*EGO!* If you've been confusing confidence and ego, you might be concerned as you read phrases such as: "Don't limit your dreams," or "You can feel confident all the time." Perhaps you hear a voice inside your head that warns: "I don't think that you should try to build up your confidence. If you do, you'll just have a big ego, and being humble all the time is much better."

If you've ever had these thoughts, you may have been brought up with a strong belief system that has actually inhibited your ability to feel confident. Did your parents ever chastise you for "bragging"? Did you get the message, either verbally or nonverbally, that thinking too highly of yourself was wrong? Were you taught that taking pride in what you accomplished would make others (your brothers, sisters, or friends) feel badly, and that it was better to be self-effacing? If you answered yes to any of these questions, you might have a difficult time really loving and honoring yourself.

❦   ❦   ❦   ❦

Many years ago, before I met my husband, I was involved in a relationship with someone who would get very uncomfortable whenever I would express my confidence. For instance, I'd be in the middle of writing an article, and he'd ask me how it was going.

"It's turning out wonderfully," I'd respond. "I think it's one of the best things I've ever written."

I'd notice my boyfriend getting a funny look on his face, and when I'd ask him what was wrong, he'd answer by telling me I sounded arrogant for being so confident. The same thing would occur when I'd return home from giving a speech and would share how powerful it had been. "How can you talk that way about yourself?" he'd ask in an aggravated voice. "You sound so stuck up."

It took many months of discussion, sometimes very heated, for me to figure out why my partner was reacting so violently to my expressions of self-confidence. As he slowly opened up to me, he revealed that, as a child, he'd been given very strong, negative messages about showing any sense of self-worth. Whenever he demonstrated any feelings of confidence, he was told to "stop showing off."

Whenever he spoke highly of himself, his father would admonish him for being a "smart mouth," and would wash his mouth out with soap. His mother would stand quietly by, never interfering, and later, would gently but clearly tell him, "We're just trying to teach you to be humble, darling. No one likes a person who is stuck up and thinks too highly of himself."

If you can relate to this story, you may be hesitant to tap into your own source of confidence for fear that you will appear to have a big ego to others. It's important, then, to understand the difference between ego and confidence.

Being confident is not the same thing as having an over-inflated ego. Being confident means believing in yourself. Ego means having to prove you're better than others.

Think of some people you know who seem to have what might be called "an ego problem." You know the kind of individuals I'm talking about—those who are always name-dropping, listing their accomplishments when you don't even ask about them, people who make sure to let you know how much money they're making, or what new, expensive possessions they just purchased. When you're around these types of people, you think to yourself, Boy, they think they're such hot stuff!

Is this kind of person truly confident? The answer is: NO! In fact, not only are they *not* confident, they are just the opposite. **Ego is always a way for people to compensate for feelings of low self-esteem. When people have to constantly advertise how wonderful they are, they are actually demonstrating how "*not* wonderful" they feel**. When people have to talk endlessly about how great they are, they aren't just trying to convince you, they're also trying to convince themselves.

Beware of Those Who Brag

I'll never forget the disastrous experience my friend Jo Anne (not her real name) had with a man who exhibited the characteristics described above:

> She had just moved to New York City after finishing college and went to work in a large advertising firm. Jo Anne wasn't the most naive person in the world, but she wasn't exactly sophisticated either. There

was a handsome senior account exec-
utive whom she noticed the first week
on the job, and she was instantly
attracted to the assured way in which
he carried himself. "Now there's a
strong, powerful man," she concluded.

It wasn't long before she was for-
mally introduced to Jason at an office
party, and he just blew Jo Anne away.
Within the first ten minutes of meeting her, he made sure she knew how
much money he was making, that he
was up for an important promotion,
that he owned a weekend house in
the country, that his ex-girlfriend still
wasn't over him, and that he had a
hard time finding a woman who
could keep up with him in bed!
Jason's onslaught of accomplishments left poor Jo Anne breathless,
and she called me in California that
night after the party.

"Doesn't he sound incredible?"
she swooned, after repeating their
conversation word for word.

Oh, yeah, I thought secretly to myself, he sounds incredibly obnoxious and insecure. And I wondered how many months Jo Anne would have to spend with Jason until she discovered the inevitable.

I didn't have to wait long to find out. One month later, she called again, this time sounding confused and deeply depressed. When I asked her what was wrong, she burst into tears.

"Oh, Barbara," she sobbed in anguish, "Jason turned out to be a nightmare. I thought he was so strong, so together, but the truth is, he's the opposite. He worries neurotically about how everything in his life will turn out. He's always comparing himself to someone richer and more successful. He doesn't even enjoy what he has, because he's afraid it's not good enough. He can't stand any feedback or criticism."

"What about the two of you?" I asked. "Did he at least treat you well?"

"The strange thing was that he felt threatened, even by me," she confessed. "And that whole story about how great he was in bed..." Jo Anne's voice lowered until I could hardly hear her. *"He was a disaster.* I didn't know whether to laugh or cry."

Poor Jo Anne had misinterpreted Jason's egotism as a strong sense of confidence, something he sorely lacked. **Like many people who don't have a true connection to their confidence, Jason tried to compensate for his sense of powerlessness by incessantly talking about how powerful he was— a sure sign that he was lacking a real belief in himself.**

⅔   ⅔   ⅔   ⅔

So, you don't have to worry that you'll finish this book and walk around turning people off with the attitude: "Okay, I feel confident, I can do anything. I am terrific." That would be obnoxious! We're looking at ways you can transform your relationship to yourself so that you are connected to a source of integrity and strength within you at all times. When you live with this kind of confidence, you will be an inspiration to others.

Taking the First Step Now

Here's the good news: You can increase your feeling of confidence within a few minutes, even within a few seconds—**all you have to do is accomplish something that brings you one step closer to one of your goals, and your confidence will instantly grow. The moment you take even the first step of action towards achieving a dream, your sense of confidence will begin expanding, because you'll trust that you can count on yourself. The more steps you take, the better you'll feel about yourself because you are DOING, and that new confidence will help you create even better results.**

Let's say your goal is that you want to learn how to operate a computer. You've been putting off buying one because you're scared that you won't be able to figure it out. It all seems overwhelming to you. And you know that with a computer, your work will be made so much easier, but the fear has been paralyzing you, perhaps for months, even years. If you sit around waiting for the fear to go away, you'll be the only person left on the block who's computer illiterate, *because the fear will not disappear until your experience changes*. What's the solution? Just take one step. Make a list of friends who have computers, and set up appointments to talk with them about their experience. Visit a computer store, and have someone give you a demonstration. Ask a colleague to give you a lesson on his or her computer.

The moment you take action, your fear will diminish, and a sense of confidence will begin to build—confidence that stems not just from your ability to be a great computer genius, but confidence in your ability to take action towards your goal.

✗   ✗   ✗   ✗

Remember, true confidence is born of your belief in your own integrity, your commitment that whatever you want, you're going to work hard to achieve it. You may not know *how* to achieve it, or even feel certain that you *will* achieve it. But when you know and trust that you will do whatever it takes, one step at a time, no matter how many mistakes you make along the way, and no matter how much fear you feel, then you've already won. In that moment, you will begin to tap into an infinite source of personal power that will fill you with more confidence than you could have ever imagined!

CHAPTER FOUR

WHY IT'S DIFFICULT TO BREAK FREE OF THE LOW SELF-ESTEEM HABIT

**Have you ever thought about
the benefits you receive in your
life by not being confident?**

**Have you ever considered the
possibility that you unconsciously
believe you're getting more out of
having low self-esteem than you
would out of having a lot of confidence?**

**Have you ever pondered what
you would lose if you suddenly
were brimming with confidence?**

Before you decide that I must have lost my mind, think about this: one of the reasons it is difficult for us, as human beings, to change unhealthy habits or negative behavior, is that we are actually getting many payoffs, or benefits, from that behavior. These aren't benefits you consciously think about, or admit to, but believe me, they're there.

Let's say that I'm in a very destructive relationship with a man, and I know I should leave, but I don't. Month after month, in spite of my unhappiness, I find myself unable to break up with my mate, and I can't figure out why. What's missing from my understanding is my emotional investment in staying—the unconscious benefits I'm receiving from being in an unhappy relationship. For instance, by staying in a miserable relationship:

I receive constant sympathy and attention from my friends.

I have a permanent excuse for why I can't concentrate on my career.

I have an excuse to overeat and indulge in bad health habits.

I can avoid looking at my issues because I'm too busy blaming my partner for being the bad guy.

So, although at first glance, it may look like I have no reason at all to remain in this unhealthy situation, you can see that there are all kinds of subtle psychological payoffs I receive by not making a change.

This same principle holds true for those of us who walk around with a lack of confidence, complaining about our low self-esteem.

No matter how much you insist you truly
want to feel good about yourself, you
may be unconsciously addicted
to some of the benefits or
payoffs you receive by playing
the role of someone who
isn't very confident.

Here's a partial list of some of the added benefits you can expect when you live life as if you have
no confidence:

You get people to feel sorry for you.

*You get people to be your motivators and cheer-
leaders, since they're always trying to build you up.*

*You avoid having people dislike you, since you
don't threaten anyone, and therefore they don't
see you as competition.*

*You get to avoid failure, since you usually don't
attempt to do much of anything.*

*You get to have a built-in excuse for any
unpleasant behavior or habit, since everyone
knows that you don't feel good about yourself.*

You get lots of attention and compliments from people, in their attempt to make you feel good about yourself.

And the list goes on...

Are You an Expert at Feeling Insecure and Inadequate?

At a seminar I gave recently, I was talking about the "payoffs" we receive from living with a lack of confidence, and a young man said something that really struck a chord with a lot of the other audience members. He remarked, *"The more I hear you talk about this issue, the more it sounds like it feels so good to feel so bad, because then you don't have to be responsible for your choices."*

I couldn't have said it better myself. And, you know what? An awful lot of us are experts—professionals almost—at suffering. You know what I mean, don't you? Think about the times when you've indulged in your depression, and you'll probably have to admit that you were really good at it. Maybe, at the time, it was the only thing that you were doing with any expertise in your life. So, why not persist in that behavior? It's human nature to enjoy doing what you're really proficient at. In fact, if you could get paid for it, you'd probably be making a great salary. (Some people do just that—I think they're called soap opera writers!)

One of the biggest payoffs you receive by living without confidence is that you have a permanent excuse for being lazy and not doing anything. When you walk around saying, "I'm having a self-esteem crisis," you're not expected to perform well. As long as you're in your "depression," or your "slump," or your "crazy time"—we all have different ways to describe it—then you don't have to do anything, do you? Your excuse for inactivity is the "state" that you're in. You don't have to act, you don't have to take risks, and therefore, you don't get to disappoint yourself or other people. And since no one expects much of you, when you do deliver, it's a big deal.

If, on the other hand, you take a risk, you may disappoint yourself; if you take a risk, you may disappoint someone else. *If you don't have the confidence to take action quite yet, you aren't going to disappoint anybody. But you* are *going to live a disappointing life*.

As human beings, we naturally feel sorry for somebody who's kind of struggling and can't get it together. We're not going to pressure them, nor are we going to make demands on them. We're going to say, "Oh, look at that poor person who can't even walk; he's falling on the ground; I won't expect anything from him." But then we see the person who's running, and who keeps tripping, and we say, "Oh, look, what a clumsy oaf." *The runner gets the criticism, and the poor crawler gets the sympathy.* So a lot of us spend our lives crawling around, convincing ourselves that we're somehow okay. Secretly, we dream of running, but we're afraid that if we run, we're going to trip, and people will notice, so we just slither along.

Walking around with low self-confidence has another enormous "benefit": it's a sure way to hook people into trying to make you feel better, especially rescuers and caretaker types who are just looking for someone to fix—you! The better you are at playing "Poor me!," the more attention and love you'll receive. The problem is that you'll never trust this kind of love, since it's based on your being a victim. This can be a really difficult psychological habit to break because *the worse you feel about yourself, the more attention you get, and the more you're "hooked" into having no confidence in order to keep getting loved.* "If I'm not a mess," your unconscious mind concludes, "no one will feel obligated to love me." So what motivation do you have for suddenly becoming strong, confident, and competent?

Some people don't know how to get love except by falling apart and hoping to be rescued. You may have seen one of your parents do this when you were a child, and think that's what love is. Or this may be the only way you received attention as a child, especially if you had absent, self-centered, addicted, or very dysfunctional parents. Being strong and confident probably got you ignored, and so you unconsciously conclude that in order to be loved, you can't feel good about yourself.

If you haven't been living with as much confidence as you'd like, ask yourself: **What are the payoffs I get from saying that I have a lack of confidence?** Make a payoff list, such as the one I presented earlier. Take an honest look at the psychological investment you may have in playing the role of someone who isn't a confident, powerful person. Perhaps you only play that role in one area of your life, such as in your intimate relationships. Maybe in your professional life, you display a lot of confidence. Don't avoid looking at the area you need to work on by pointing out to yourself how successful you are in the area you've already mastered!

The unconscious motivations we've been looking at can be difficult to spot and even harder to accept. Sometimes you've been playing these roles for so long that you don't even realize what you're doing, or how harmful these habits are in the long run. **In the end, however, negative payoffs don't pay off!** The love, the attention, the refuge from risk and failure they give you are all temporary illusions. They will not fill your heart or nourish your spirit. They ultimately take away your power, instead of strengthening it. Letting go of the old habits and roles takes courage, but the true sense of confidence you gain will reward you in more ways than you can imagine!

⚞   ⚞   ⚞   ⚞

C H A P T E R   F I V E

MASTERING THE THREE TYPES OF CONFIDENCE

Now it's time to look more deeply at how you can begin to experience powerful, new levels of confidence in your life. There are actually three types of confidence that we all need to develop: *behavioral confidence, emotional confidence,* and *spiritual confidence.* All three are necessary for you to become the powerful and fulfilled person you deserve to be.

Behavioral confidence means **confidence in your ability to act and get things done in your life,** whether it's something as simple as paying the bills on time, or something more esoteric like making your dreams come true. That is one kind of confidence. When most of us think of developing confidence, it's behavioral confidence we are striving for.

The second type of confidence is what I call *emotional confidence.* **Emotional confidence is your belief and your ability to master your emotional world:** to know what you are feeling, to make the right emotional choices in your life, to protect yourself from pain, to know how to create a healthy, lasting relationship. Some of us have a lot of behavioral confidence, and therefore, we've achieved a certain level of success, but we have low emotional confidence and are unhappy in our personal lives.

On the other hand, some of us have very high levels of emotional confidence, but we can't even hold down a job for one day.

The third kind of confidence is actually the most important, and I call it *spiritual confidence.* **Spiritual confidence is your trust in the Universe,** your conviction that life will have a positive outcome, your belief that you are here for a reason, and that there is a purpose to your 70 or 80 or 90 years spent on this planet. Without spiritual confidence, I believe that, ultimately, it is difficult to truly develop the other two kinds of confidence—behavioral and emotional.

Before we discuss how to understand and develop these three kinds of confidence, take a moment right now to look at your life objectively, and ask yourself *if one of these three areas is stronger in you than the other two.* Perhaps you have a successful business and have learned how to push past your fear of failure in that area, but you've had a series of painful, unfulfilling relationships and can't seem to find the right mate. Perhaps you are happily married with children, but can't seem to persevere long enough to get a successful career going, and are always struggling to make ends meet. Or, maybe, you feel weak in all three areas!

**Becoming a confident person means
developing your confidence equally
in all three areas—behavioral,
emotional and spiritual—so that
you're living a life that is
balanced as well as powerful.**

How to Develop Behavioral Confidence

When you possess behavioral confidence, you feel confident that you will do everything it takes, to the best of your ability, in order to help your life and your activities turn out the way that you want them to. Here are four important characteristics associated with behavioral confidence:

1. **The belief in your ability to take action.**

   For example, if your dream is to start your own business, behavioral confidence for you would be the belief that you are going to take action to achieve this goal, instead of just talking about it for the next five years. It means you trust yourself to put together a business plan, to educate yourself about the process of running your own company, and to create a time line that defines the birth and development of your new venture.

If your goal is to strengthen your marriage, behavioral confidence would mean that you trust yourself to have meaningful conversations with your husband, to make mutual commitments to improving your relationship, and to acquire helpful tools and techniques that you can both begin using on a regular basis.

2. **The belief in your ability to follow through with your actions and be consistent.**

Do you ever start things but just don't get around to finishing them? Do you spread yourself in so many directions that you can't get anything done to completion? Many of us take the first few steps of action towards achieving a goal, but stop before fulfilling the task, either because we're afraid to go further, or because we become overwhelmed, or because we're disorganized and unfocused. Behavioral confidence means you will not only plan and begin important actions, but that you *will* follow through.

3. **The belief in your ability to push through obstacles**.

Some of us are great at moving forward in life when things are smooth, but we stop in our tracks when obstacles arise. Do you have a low tolerance for obstacles? Any path worth traveling is going to be fraught with obstacles. So, real behavioral confidence requires a belief in your ability to handle obstacles. That means that when you come up against a challenge or obstruction in your path, you won't exclaim, "Oh, my God," and bury your face in a carton of ice cream, or spend the next few days in bed. It's the belief that, instead, you are going to say, "Aha! An obstacle—I was expecting this!" And then you'll rally your forces.

And finally:

4. The belief in your ability to ask for help.

Many of us stubbornly think that we have to make our dreams come true by ourselves, and that if we ask for help, our success somehow doesn't count. This is one of the worst ways in which you can sabotage yourself and your sense of confidence. I used to be very guilty of this. "I have to do it alone," I'd complain. "I can't count on anybody." So I would do it alone, whatever it was, and at the same time, I'd complain that no one would help me. The truth was, I wouldn't *let* anyone help me. I wouldn't give any responsibility away. As a result, I was resentful, overworked, and unhappy. When I realized that behavioral confidence meant that I trusted myself to ask for help when I needed it, I began reaching out to others for support. An amazing thing happened: my business improved 100 percent.

Do *you* ever have a hard time asking for help? Do you feel you have to do it all by yourself? You've got to change that attitude if you want to expand your sense of confidence. *Asking for help is not a sign of weakness; it is a sign of intelligence and a sign of self-love.*

Those are the four characteristics associated with behavioral confidence. When you lack one or more of them, your behavior will reflect a lack of confidence, and that lack of confidence will manifest itself in particular patterns. If you exhibit any of the four symptoms that follow, you probably need to strengthen your behavioral confidence.

1. You *procrastinate* about getting started.

2. You *overanalyze* your options with

respect to the pros and cons of doing things without actually committing to a decision. You may vacillate so much that by the time you finally do make a decision, you've lost your sense of passion and purpose for the goal.

3. You *avoid the real challenging issues* in your life, and focus on issues that don't really need attention.

4. You *mask your need for help* from others in difficult situations (whether at home or at work) by telling people that everything is okay.

If you can relate to any of the above statements, or intuitively know that you need more behavioral confidence, here are a few suggestions that can help:

1. Write down specific, small steps of action for every dream you have, including a time line with deadlines.

That means that instead of saying, "I want to open my own consulting business," and then sitting around every day feeling overwhelmed, you create small, achievable goals. For instance, you say, "This week, I want to make one phone call a day to someone in a similar business." Breaking down your big goal into small steps and taking them one after another, is a wonderful way of giving yourself more behavioral confidence.

2. Seek out successful people, and learn from them.

A lot of us don't want to associate with successful people because we're secretly, or not so secretly, jealous of them. So we tend to hang around other people who are jealous of successful people, and just enhance our own negativity and limited thinking. *I suggest that you find people who have achieved what you are striving for, whether it is a successful business, or a successful marriage, or whatever, and learn from them.* Find opportunities to talk with them. Ask them out to lunch. Invite them to share their greatest insights and most valuable lessons. You will find that associating with people whom you admire will uplift you, inspire you, and increase your behavioral confidence.

3. **Make a list of people you can go to for help and support.**

You'd be surprised how many people you know, or your friends and acquaintances know, who would be happy to help you achieve your goals and make your dreams come true. Create a list of resources, so that whenever you are feeling overwhelmed, you can pick up the phone, or send an E-mail message, and get the extra encouragement you need.

Remember: the most important key to developing behavioral confidence is to keep taking action. The more you trust yourself to go forward, the more confidence you'll feel.

How to Develop Emotional Confidence

When you possess emotional confidence, you have a strong belief in your ability to master your inner world of emotions. Here are five important characteristics associated with emotional confidence.

1. **The belief in your ability to know your own feelings.**

    Being able to identify what you are feeling *when* you are feeling it is an important component of emotional confidence. So many of us walk around with all sorts of emotions erupting in our hearts, but we have no idea that these feelings even exist. You can't feel emotionally confident when you look upon your emotional reality as some sort of mystery you don't know how to figure out. And you certainly can't have healthy relationships without this quality of emotional confidence.

2. **The belief in your ability to express your own feelings, to get what is inside out.**

   Knowing what you are feeling is just the first step in being emotionally confident. The second is being able to express those feelings appropriately to the people involved, whether it be your lover, your friend, your sister, or your son. Unexpressed emotions stagnate inside our hearts, creating emotional blockages that prevent us from being able to give or receive love.

3. **The belief in your ability to connect with other human beings in a loving and meaningful way.**

   We live in a world populated by over five billion people, and learning to connect with our fellow travelers is a necessary part of developing emotional confidence. It's impossible to feel confident if you're afraid to go to a party, or a business meeting, or a social gathering, because you aren't sure how to interact with people in a meaningful way. Trusting in your ability to connect with others in a way that serves you both will increase your emotional confidence and contribute a lot more love and fulfillment to your life.

4. **The belief in your ability to find love, understanding, and compassion in all situations, especially difficult ones**.

   One of the keys to creating successful relationships, and therefore, one of the keys to creating emotional confidence, is the ability to process yourself through unpleasant emotions until you arrive back at a place of love and understanding. Life is destined to bombard you with many difficult personal challenges and a myriad of intense emotions—from anger to grief and everything in between. *It's not enough to just know how you feel, or even to express it. You must have the confidence that you can navigate through the maze of your feelings and get to your deepest truth. You must cultivate the habit of looking for the love, the bigger purpose, and the real meaning in all situations.* When you have the confidence that you can do so, you won't feel like a victim of your emotions, or of the events happening to you and around you, but rather, you will feel anchored to a source of compassion and clarity deep within.

5. **The belief in your ability to know that what you have to offer others as a human being is valuable**.

   You are one of a kind. There is no one else exactly like you in the world; there never has been, and there never will be again. Knowing who you are and what you have to offer is part of feeling emotionally confident. When you understand and honor your uniqueness, you will realize how valuable you are to everyone who knows you. *You are necessary. What you have to give is necessary.*

Those are the five characteristics associated with emotional confidence. Perhaps you've developed several of them, and are still working on others. Perhaps reading about them and admitting that these qualities are lacking in your life has helped you realize why you don't feel emotionally confident. When you don't feel a strong sense of emotional confidence, you might exhibit the following symptoms:

1. You frequently *numb yourself to your feelings* and don't seem to know what's going on in your life. You say, "I'm so confused" a lot. Many of us hang out in confusion as a way to protect ourselves. As long as we're confused, we don't have to be held accountable for how we feel. *Confusion usually covers up some unpleasant emotions we'd rather not deal with.*

2. You *edit your feelings,* and don't hon-
    estly express them to other people. You
    may keep people guessing about how
    you feel, which is a subtle way of con-
    trolling them. No one really knows the
    real you, and who you are on the inside
    is quite different from who people see
    on the outside.

3. You isolate *yourself.* When you don't
    have the confidence to connect with
    others in a meaningful way, you isolate
    yourself from social situations and
    tend to live in a personal world with
    very limiting boundaries.

4. You are a *people pleaser and an
    approval junkie.* Since you don't pos-
    sess your own emotional confidence,
    you desperately need other people's
    approval to validate you and define
    your self-worth.

5. You are *judgmental and practice nega-
    tivity thinking.* You tend to criticize
    that which you do not understand or
    feel controlled by. Without emotional

confidence, you may feel overwhelmed by your emotions and the
effect that others have on you. Your
only defense might be to protect yourself by attacking the person or situation with negative thoughts and judg-
ments. *The more disempowered people
are, the more judgmental they will be.*

*If any of these symptoms seem to be describing
you, or if you just want to develop more emotional
confidence, here are some suggestions that can help:*

1. Learn to identify and resolve your feelings.

Don't ever settle for telling yourself,
"I don't know what I'm feeling." Instead,
say, "All right, I know I'm feeling something, because I'm uncomfortable. I'll
just sit here until I figure it out, or I'll call
someone to help me." Find tools and
techniques that can teach you how to get
in touch with your emotions, and express
them effectively and appropriately. Use
my *Making Love Work* (© 1993) system,
or someone else's system, or create your
own, but *don't just stay emotionally*

unconscious. Each time you work through your emotions, instead of suppressing them, your emotional confidence will grow.

2. Learn how to express your feelings to others.

This is an extension of the first suggestion. *Hiding your emotions from others only serves to build emotional walls between you, and create a sense of distance and disconnection.* Don't put off talking about the things you need to address in your relationships. Facing your issues, instead of running away from them, will strengthen your emotional confidence.

3. Create opportunities for connection with other people.

Don't isolate yourself. It's one of the worst ways to sabotage your emotional confidence. You can't learn how to feel good about yourself and others when you are alone at home. Reach out to your friends and loved ones. Show them the person you really are inside. If you don't have many acquaintances, join groups that bring people together—volunteer organizations, support groups, service groups. The more that you're around human beings, being genuinely yourself, the more emotional confidence you'll experience.

Remember: emotional confidence is something you can only develop on the inside. The more you connect with and honor what is inside your heart, the more emotionally confident you will feel, and the more powerfully you'll be able to relate to others.

How to Develop Spiritual Confidence

You've probably never heard the term *spiritual confidence* before now. I believe that this is the most important kind of confidence there is, because it defines your relationship with the Universe you live in. Here are three characteristics associated with spiritual confidence.

1. The belief that the Universe is a constantly evolving mystery, and that there is a universal flow towards good.

Everywhere you look in the natural world, you will observe that all life is designed to evolve. An infant magically grows into an adult, a seed grows into a tree. Built into each physical manifestation, whether it's a cell, a forest, or a human being, is an innate intelligence that guides the living organism to develop and express itself more fully. You are part of that mystery, part of the inevitable flow towards more.

Spiritual confidence comes from understanding the positive direction in which the Universe is going, and trust-

ing that, although you may not always see how, your life is going in the same direction.

2. The belief in the order of the Universe—that it makes sense.

If you feel like you're living in a crazy world with no rules, you won't have much spiritual confidence. Everything will appear to happen randomly, and you'll feel a constant sense of insecurity. Spiritual confidence develops when you observe the cycles of nature and the mechanics of creation, and conclude that our reality has been designed by an ordering intelligence beyond anything you or I can imagine. This all-pervasive intelligence is obvious in the tiniest detail of a bird's feather, all the way to the rotation of the planets.

When you begin to perceive universal truths that explain your perceptions and experience, spiritual confidence begins growing inside you. You know that even your greatest challenges must, like all things in nature, have a purpose—otherwise they wouldn't be happening.

3. **The belief in yourself as a miraculous expression of God, Spirit, Higher Intelligence, or whatever great force you feel is responsible for creation.**

If you think about it, your very existence is a miracle. Somehow, you know yourself as the person you are; somehow, your consciousness lives within your physical body, learning, feeling, growing, loving. Somehow, you are here, visiting this place we call Earth. *You are a unique, one-of-a-kind expression of whomever or whatever created all that is and all that ever will be. Isn't that a miracle?*

As an expression of the whole, you have within you the same magnificence you see when you gaze up at a mountain; you have within you the same beauty you witness when you watch a sunset; you have within you the same power as that which created you in the first place. *Spiritual confidence comes from remembering who you really are, beyond your body and personality, beyond the masks you wear. It comes from honoring yourself as one of creation's miracles.*

When you are lacking in spiritual confidence, you might experience the following symptoms:

1. You try to *control everything* in your life. *You* have to be in control because you don't trust God, or the Universe, to create a positive outcome. This mistrust often immobilizes you from taking action, or sabotages your relationships when you refuse to fully open up. You find it hard to flow with events and experiences, and by resisting, you make your life more dramatic and painful than it needs to be.

2. You have a *difficult time being adventurous or taking risks*. When you don't have confidence that the Universe operates in an orderly, meaningful fashion, you don't feel safe. You behave, love, and work cautiously. *You live a more limited, protected, uninspired life, and therefore, a less fulfilling life.*

3. You feel a *deep sense of emotional restlessness*. Nothing completely satisfies you. Nothing fills you up. That's because you're waiting for life to validate you, to give you a reason for being here; therefore, you are missing the point: *the fact that you are here at all means you are a miracle. You are loved. You are enough.*

Here are some suggestions for developing spiritual confidence:

1. Seek out evidence that the Universe operates in an orderly, positive fashion.

Look back on your life and the life

of others, and see how many times situations you thought were problems
turned out to be blessings in disguise.
Remember a time when you thought,
"I am never going to love anyone ever
again," and you did; recall a time when
you found a door closing to you, only
to reveal another opening. See how life
is constantly growing.

2. **Spend time outdoors in Nature, and
   pay attention to what you see.**

   Nature is an ever-present and powerful spiritual teacher. When you walk
through a grove of trees, or stare at the
details of a flower, or watch the
ocean's waves crash onto the shore, or
look up at the stars filling the night
sky, you will instantly notice and connect with the magnificent, unlimited
intelligence that is responsible for all
of creation. The more you observe the
wonders of our physical existence, the
easier it will be for you to experience
spiritual confidence.

3. Look for everyday miracles and evidence that you are loved.

Every day, you are surrounded by signs that remind you of how blessed you are to be alive. Every day, you will receive evidence that you are loved. The sun will rise to light your way and give you warmth. The earth will bring forth food to nourish you. Just when you are feeling sad, a bird will begin to sing. Just when you are feeling totally alone, a child will smile at you. Just when you are feeling that you cannot figure out what to do with a problem, the answer will come: you'll bump into the right person, or read the right book, or suddenly, have the right revelation. Look for evidence that you are being guided and watched over. Look for evidence that *you are loved.*

꘎   ꘎   ꘎   ꘎

Ultimately, spiritual confidence is a quiet, gentle sense of peace. It fills your heart and nurtures your spirit. It allows you to travel your path knowing that you are on the right road, and trusting that wherever you are is just where you need to be....

꘎   ꘎   ꘎   ꘎

❧ EPILOGUE ❧

Know these things, then, and feel confident:

You have everything you need inside of you right
now to live the life you are dreaming of.

❧

Any lack of confidence you feel is simply an illu-
sion. You are a magnificent, perfect child of the
Universe. You are powerful beyond measure.

❧

The more you love yourself and enjoy this life, the
more you honor that which created you.

❧

The more you manifest your true beauty and
express your unique gift, the more the Universe
will rejoice.

❧

That's why you are here—to be as extraordinarily
outrageous a "you" as possible.

What are you waiting for?

✄ ABOUT THE AUTHOR ✄

Barbara De Angelis, Ph.D., is an internationally recognized expert on human relations and one of America's most influential teachers in the area of personal and spiritual development. She is the author of numerous bestselling books, including *Real Moments, Secrets About Men Every Woman Should Know, Are You the One for Me?* and *How to Make Love All the Time.* Barbara has hosted her own television and radio shows, as well as appearing for several years on CNN as their Newsnight Relationship Expert. Her television infomercial, *MAKING LOVE WORK*, is the most successful relationship program of its kind. Barbara is known for sharing her warmth, vitality, and inspirational presence with her audiences.

We hope
you enjoyed
this Hay House book.
If you would like to receive a
free catalog featuring additional
Hay House books and products, or if
you would like information
about the Hay Foundation,
please contact:

Hay House, Inc.
P.O. Box 5100
Carlsbad, CA 92018-5100

(800) 654-5126
(800) 650-5115 (fax)

Please visit the Hay House Website at:
www.hayhouse.com